I0418168

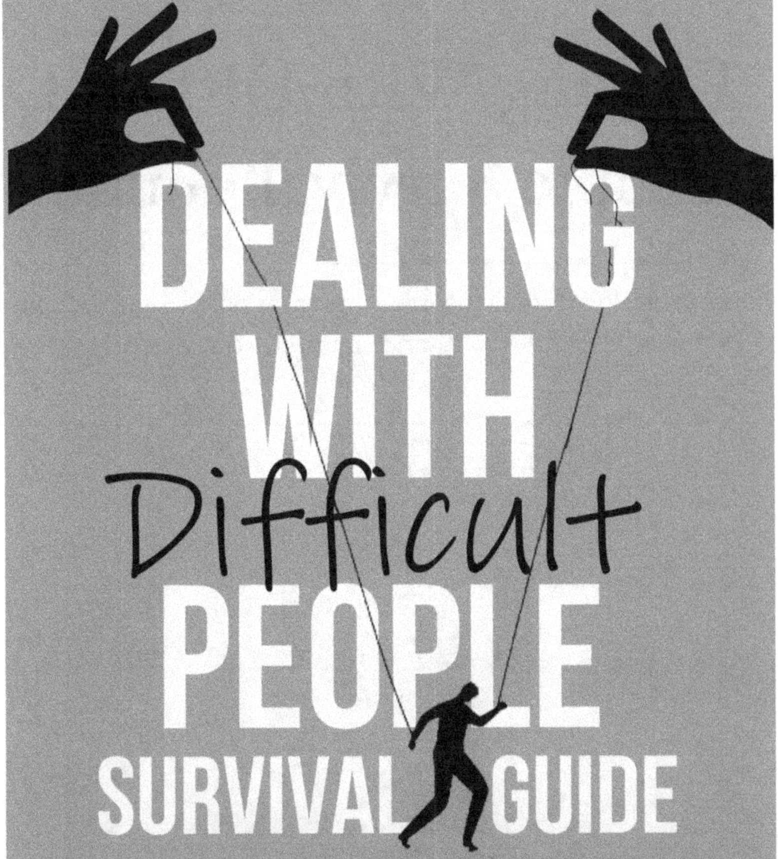

DEALING WITH Difficult PEOPLE
SURVIVAL GUIDE

HOW TO DEAL WITH TOXIC PEOPLE WITH EMOTIONAL REGULATION AND 235 POWERFUL PHRASES TO DISARM MANIPULATORS, NARCISSISTS, AND GASLIGHTING

ROBERT J. CHARLES, PHD, DMIN

Dealing With Difficult People Survival Guide

How to deal with toxic people with emotional regulation and 235 powerful phrases to disarm manipulators, narcissists, and gaslighting

Robert J. Charles

Copyright © 2023 by Robert J. Charles - All rights reserved.

The content contained within this book may not be reproduced, duplicated, or transmitted without direct written permission from the author or the publisher.

Under no circumstances will any blame or legal responsibility be held against the publisher, or author, for any damages, reparation, or monetary loss due to the information contained within this book. Either directly or indirectly. You are responsible for your own choices, actions, and results.

Legal Notice:

This book is copyright protected. This book is only for personal use. You cannot amend, distribute, sell, use, quote, or paraphrase any part of the content within this book without the consent of the author or publisher.

Disclaimer Notice:

Please note the information contained within this document is for educational and entertainment purposes only. All effort has been executed to present accurate, up-to-date, and reliable, complete information. No warranties of any kind are declared or implied. Readers acknowledge that the author is not engaging in the rendering of legal, financial, medical, or professional advice. The content within this book has been derived from various sources. Please consult a licensed professional before attempting any techniques outlined in this book.

By reading this document, the reader agrees that under no circumstances is the author responsible for any losses, direct or indirect, which are incurred as a result of the use of the information contained within this document, including, but not limited to, — errors, omissions, or inaccuracies.

Contents

DO YOU WANT TO OVERCOME OVERTHINKING?

These **3 FREE** offers are exactly for you: 2 audiobooks + 1 e-book.

You will also get the 'Dealing with Difficult People' audiobook.

<u><<Just click right here to discover the physical effects of overthinking on your skin, immune system, and well-being>></u>

In these 2 audiobooks and 1 e-book, YOU will discover:

- The three different forms of overthinking and how to spot them.
- How ruminating and worries can damage your social life.
- The types of toxic people and how to escape their web of crises.
- How to Discover If You Are a Highly Sensitive Person and ways to deal with that.

If you want to finally stop overthinking,
<u>Click here to get these 3 FREE offers.</u>

1

OTHER BONUS

How to Face any Challenge with Confidence?

Download these **FREE 30 BIBLICAL PROMISES** to discover some powerful promises for **YOU**.

Click: https://go.robertjcharles.com/30BiblicalPromises

At some point, everyone on this Earth faces a tough challenge. Help is on the way! God has your back. His Word will empower you to face any trial or tribulation. These 30 promises from God will give you the strength and resilience you need to move forward.

To get your **FREE** 30 BIBLICAL PROMISES TO OVERCOME ANY CHALLENGE, **click on this link:**

https://go.robertjcharles.com/30BiblicalPromises

Introduction

Y ou have probably heard the story of the frog in the boiling pot of water many times. But in case you haven't, here it is: An unlucky frog falls into a pot of warm water. The pot is still on the stove with the burner on. At this point, anyone would expect the frog to leap out of the water and get as far away as it can from danger. But the frog does not.

The water temperature starts to rise. The frog still doesn't budge. Instead, it manages to regulate its body temperature accordingly.

However, as the water in the pot approaches the boiling point, the frog is no longer able to keep up and regulate its body temperature. It attempts to jump out of the pot of water but is unable to do so since the water has already reached the boiling point.

Come on! Something has to give, right?

Of course, the frog dies.

It sounds cruel, but the frog dies. What happened? Do you blame the hot water for the frog's death? What was responsible for the frog's death? The reality is, the frog died a fool's death. All along, it could have simply jumped out of that deathtrap before it got too hot. But it didn't.

The frog kept adjusting its body temperature to cope with the rising temperature. The more the temperature increased, the more the frog adjusted. It continued to cope this way until the temperature became unbearable. At this point, the frog tried to escape, but it was already too late. The frog had expended all of its energy trying to survive in an unfavorable environment until it could no longer make it out alive. Instead of deploying its energy to save itself, the frog chose to deploy its energy unwisely, and as a result, it died.

Like so many people out there, you might be the little frog. You feel relaxed and undisturbed in the face of mounting toxicity and just lie back while other people manipulate you, letting them dish out all their negative energy on you.

Your boss talks to you like trash, continually humiliates you in front of other employees, and dumps his excess workload on you. Among your colleagues at work, you are the subject of every joke. No one ever recognizes the amount of effort you put into your job. Even worse, they take credit for your ideas and make sure you always take the fall when things go south. You just lie back and take it.

Your neighbors have made your house a living nightmare and seem to never run out of ideas to get on your nerves. They turn up the music volume at night when you're trying to get some rest. They trash your yard at will, and always encroach on your property. These jerks even make fun of you when you try to talk to them. They call you a crybaby and dare you to do your worst. You just lie back and take it.

You just take all of their toxicity. You never challenge these manipulators. You never draw a line. You never say STOP! Just like the frog, you remain right there amid all that toxicity.

At your place of work, you cope with abuse by seeing yourself as a team player. You consider yourself an invaluable link in the smooth running of the organization. So, you accept all the abuse, and you stay.

At home, you live like a ghost. You're afraid of standing up to your noisy neighbors or even letting them see you. You assume that it's best to ignore them for the sake of peace. So, you accept all the stress, and you stay.

Just like the frog, you stay. Never moving. You just stay. You consider yourself strong and resilient. You consider your skin thick enough. Well, that's where you're wrong.

Think about it. You are just one of the billions of people you share the world with. Studies show that over 70% of adults worldwide have had to deal with depression at some point in their lives. Of this 70%, only a few ever overcome the trauma they might have suffered as children.

It's a freaking circus out there. Many of the people you meet are dealing with pent-up stress and emotions. Most of them only get a bit of relief by making other people feel as miserable as they are.

Here is where it gets worse. Toxic people never stop. They will continue to unload their poison on whatever victim they find. Like a relentless viper, they will continue to strike their prey, filling it with harmful venom until the prey dies. Are you willing to risk that?

Just like the frog, there's a limit to how much toxicity you can handle. Once you reach your breaking point, things are no longer in your control.

Many people have given up on their dreams. They've given up on love. They've given up on family. As a result, many of them pick up bad habits and addictions that eventually cost them their lives in a bid to accommodate the toxic people around them and endure the toxic environment in which they find themselves. Sadly, many also take their own lives when they can no longer endure it.

Think about it: more people die from depression and stress-related diseases each year than the number of people that died during both the First and Second World Wars.

Just like the frog, most of these people accepted toxicity from the people around them. They adopted various coping mechanisms that they thought would help them get through all of that toxicity without ever setting up boundaries or confronting their manipulators head-on. They tried to thrive in the face of mounting toxicity till it cost them their health and, in some cases, ultimately, their lives.

Why would anyone want to go down the same path? Why would YOU want to go down that path? Why give up your comfort, peace of mind, and growth? Why channel your energies in the wrong direction? What point are you trying to prove? Why not take charge of your life and begin to truly thrive? Why be that frog? Why not stand up to the toxic people in your life and let them know that there are lines they are not allowed to cross? Why not ask God to give you the wisdom to deal with these people?

There's so much growth and fulfillment that you are denying yourself by letting toxic people take control of your life. You can achieve endless possibilities by taking control out of the hands of these manipulators. You can bring truly magnificent creations to life by channeling your energy positively. There's a bright new world out there where you'll be respected and your opinions will be valued, where people will recognize your boundaries and strive to maintain healthy and productive relationships with you. There's a whole new level of friendship out there that you can enjoy, my friend. This world is yours if only you are willing to take it. Are you?

In this book, you will discover:

- effective strategies successful people have used to deal with toxic people;

- helpful tips you can use to identify people with toxic traits and to shield yourself from them; and

- quick and catchy phrases that will help you overcome manipulative people.

And that's just the beginning.

This book will also show you effective measures you can take to heal from previous toxic relationships as you begin to create new and healthy ones. You'll also find real stories of people who have gone on to live truly remarkable lives after breaking the chains of toxicity around them. You can join them.

Here's the truth: you will always have to deal with toxic people. They will always try to manipulate you. Will you let them? Or will you master the skills you need to overcome them?

In this book, I share tested and trusted strategies for dealing with toxic people.

So, jump in. Master these strategies, and watch the new world you desire unfold before you.

This new world is yours, my friend. Start living in it.

PART ONE
Understanding And Benefits

CHAPTER 1

Caught In The Web

"If any of you lacks wisdom, let him ask God, who gives generously to all without reproach, and it will be given him."

– James 1:5 ESV

Did you hear what happened to Mark?

He was top of his class for three consecutive years, the valedictorian on the day of his graduation, and widely acclaimed as the kid with the most potential to succeed amongst his peers and adults alike. Mark had the world in his hands. He had it all. Well, we all thought he did.

Three years after joining one of the fastest growing insurance providers in all of America, he had become one of the most valuable salespeople the company had ever found. His promotions were so fast that it was hard to keep track of them. He was an inspiration to new employees, the envy of his colleagues, and though he did not know it, a thorn in the flesh of many senior ranking employees.

In no time, Mark was appointed as the deputy to the most senior regional director. By this time, a lot of people naturally expected him to take over this regional director's role when the old man retired the next year. However, that wasn't the case.

Like many other senior executives, Mark's new boss had heard of the new wonder kid who had ascended the corporate ladder at a rate never seen before. Although the old man had no personal misgivings about Mark's success, he saw Mark as nothing but opportunistic, not someone who was worthy to replace him.

So, with the help of other senior executives who shared his view, the regional director went about his plan. He saddled Mark with more responsibilities. It didn't matter if these tasks were far above or far beneath Mark's station. He sent Mark running on fruitless errands with no real purpose or value and set unrealistic deadlines for phantom reports and assessments. He humiliated Mark in front of his subordinates and continually trashed every idea Mark developed.

This nasty old man turned Mark's dream career into a nightmare. Mark tried his best to cope with all this toxicity. He considered it all part of the job experience. He hadn't come this far in his career by being an easy pushover. He took great pride in the thick skin he had developed over the years.

Just like so many other career professionals, Mark believed he could ride out the thunderstorms of toxicity and become a better person and employee. He believed that all the abuse he endured was a refining process, and that, like gold, he would come out of this furnace more valuable. He accepted all the abuse because he believed it was part of a learning curve that would deliver the hard lessons he was yet to learn about the industry.

Unfortunately, he was wrong. Like an old, rusty suit of armor subjected to a relentless barrage of enemy fire, Mark's thick skin started to crack. He began to find it hard to concentrate on his job. He lost the desire to share or implement any of the ideas or strategies he developed.

Once sociable and extroverted, he withdrew into a shell he'd never believed he had. Of course, it didn't take long before many people started to notice the changes. Even though these changes were glaring, Mark always insisted he was fine and that there was nothing to worry about.

He never made any complaints, confronted his abuser, nor stood up for himself. With time, he began to lose interest in his job. He started to doubt himself and questioned his life decisions. The job he had once enjoyed no longer appealed to him.

As a result, Mark became the topic of all sorts of office gossip. He was named a fraud by many of his colleagues. No longer did anyone see him as the golden kid who would turn the fortunes of the company around. Mark wasn't aware of the numerous bits of gossip flying around him—and even if he had been, at this point, he wouldn't have cared.

There are lots of Marks out there. The details might be slightly different, but they all have the same sad story surrounding their lives. They have come in contact with a lot of toxic people. Unequipped with the skills and strategies in this book, they have fallen prey to their manipulators.

Your story doesn't have to be the same as theirs because you hold the secrets right here in your hand.

In this chapter, you will learn how to identify the traits and qualities of the five most toxic personalities. With this knowledge, you can begin to identify toxic people from far away, and later in this book, you'll also learn how to deal with them. You could also use this knowledge to evaluate any existing relationships you might have with toxic people.

You will also discover effective strategies you can use to control your emotions and the way you react to toxic people. This way, you gain the upper hand over your manipulators whenever they try to unload all their toxicity on you.

This knowledge also puts you in a better position to deny them any satisfaction they might derive from seeing you succumb to their toxic venom.

The Five Kinds of Toxic People That Can Ruin Your Life

Toxic people come in different shapes and sizes. Though there are many remarkable people out there, you'll also meet some people who exhibit one form of toxicity or another. You might try to make excuses for their behavior and draw them into your close circle with the hope of changing them with time.

Well, here's the truth. Nobody is born toxic. People develop toxic behaviors due to their personal experiences.

Toxic people may have had a tough childhood. They might have lived with abusive partners. They might have worked under terrible bosses. However, the truth is that they weren't born toxic. At some point in their lives, they developed toxic behaviors to help them cope with the abuse they suffered.

With time, these behaviors became a kind of invaluable defense mechanism they couldn't do without. Unconsciously, these behaviors became a part of their lifestyle. Toxic people learn their behavior; they can unlearn it too, but unfortunately, many do not.

Toxicity moves in a vicious cycle. Toxic people pass on their toxicity to other people, who then pass on the same toxicity to even more people. If you continue to excuse their behavior, you risk continuing the vicious cycle of toxicity.

You might not be able to avoid coming in contact with toxic people, but you can break the vicious cycle. In order to do this, you must be able to identify them first.

Here's a list of five toxic people you might regularly encounter:

1. The Narcissists
2. The Paranoids

3. The Sociopaths

4. The Psychotics

5. The Histrionics

1. The Narcissists

Narcissists are people who are obsessed with themselves. They are full of themselves 101% of the time and believe that everyone around them must see them through the same twisted lens with which they view themselves.

These people believe that it's their world we are living in and that we must worship and adore them for even allowing us to exist around them.

Narcissists believe they should always be the center of attention, and will resist anyone who dares share the spotlight with them or tries to draw the tiniest bit of attention away from them. They move around with an awkward sense of entitlement and never take responsibility for their actions.

The narcissist can never be wrong. In their mind, they are always right. They must look good regardless of what it might cost. They will never apologize for any mistakes they make but blame other people instead.

In reality, narcissists are insecure people with fragile egos. They are actual nobodies who only thrive by making others around them feel small, inadequate, and unqualified.

At your place of work, narcissists will continually criticize your output and put down any ideas you come up with. A narcissistic partner will gaslight you if you try to hold them to higher standards.

It is impossible to thrive with narcissists. If you let them, they will drain you of your energy and push you into a very dark shell of yourself.

2. The Paranoids

Paranoids are very difficult people to deal with. They live in perpetual fear. They see signs, omens, and patterns everywhere, and draw unrealistic comparisons between events and happenings around them.

Since misery loves company, paranoid people do their best to draw others around them into the same fear and insecurity in which they envelop themselves. There is not much you can do about chronic paranoids. They believe that the world is against them and that there are lots of unseen, united forces out there with the common goal of thwarting all their plans.

Paranoid people never let go of any offenses they might have suffered in the past, and they project negative stereotypes from past offenders on everyone they meet. They are perpetually scared of being abandoned and will monitor their partners' lives constantly. If you don't know any better, you might even believe that their overbearing attitude and obsession with your daily activities are an excessive show of their love and admiration for you.

The fear of abandonment makes paranoids continually doubt and mistrust their partners. They will also often resort to emotional blackmail.

3. The Sociopaths

Most of the dreaded criminals whose blood-curdling records continue to stoke feelings of fear and disgust amongst members of the public are well-established sociopaths. Sociopaths are full-time antisocial souls with no regard at all for morals or societal standards. The major characteristic of sociopaths is their innate tendency to dominate the people around them.

Sociopaths take great pleasure in subjecting others to humiliation. They have no reservations about exhibiting their domineering attitude in public and publicly disgracing their partners.

It is common to find sociopaths taking time to identify any weak points you may have and then using them against you. Sociopaths are also masters of the blame game; they will always find someone else to take the fall for their failures. They have a high tendency to lie.

They also have no misgivings about stealing from others or, in some cases, even killing whoever threatens the feeble image of strength they try to portray. If you have a sociopathic partner, your self-esteem will take a sharp dive and you'll lose every bit of confidence you have in yourself. You'll lower your standards and soon discover that you're living in fear most of the time. With time, you'll resort to self-loathing and start to rely on their validation.

4. The Psychotics

Psychotic people are prone to irregular outbursts and neurotic breakdowns. Like ocean waves, their moods are volatile and often swing up and down for no reason at all. It is difficult to reason with them because they are easily triggered and can subject you to very distressing episodes on a whim, at the slightest provocation.

You will often find it impossible to hold constructive discussions with psychotics since they are prone to making incoherent speeches and get agitated at the slightest hint of criticism. Psychotic people just can't help themselves; they are usually unaware of their toxic behavior.

Plagued by unwanted thoughts, psychotic people often experience feelings of guilt and nervousness. Most of them will mistake a harmless look for an accusatory stare. They typically have very low self-esteem and are overly dependent on the validation of other people. They will often withdraw into themselves if they do not receive the adulation they greatly desire.

They frequently make excuses for their behavior and even go as far as blaming others. Often, they are unable to differentiate between reality and their frequent hallucinations or delusions. They will hold grudges for nonexistent offenses.

Continuous feelings of depression and self-loathing leave psychotic people with frequent negative thoughts, and they may engage in self-harm.

5. The Histrionics

To histrionics, drama is the very air they breathe. They love being at the center of the action and do not hesitate to create a problem where one is nonexistent. These people bask in public validation. They want to be seen, heard, felt, smelled, and talked about all the time. If they go too long without getting involved in any sort of drama, they become depressed and overly anxious.

Histrionics have no issue with stirring up controversy. They can spread false tales and even speak ill of other people just to get things started. Dealing with histrionics is very draining. You will need to put up with one drama or another on a daily basis. You'll find yourself dealing with meaningless offenses and situations that could have easily been avoided.

Oftentimes, histrionics recruit supporters to their side to back them up whenever they are confronted with their lies. They will expect you to take their side regardless of the damage they might have caused to others. Do not be surprised if they try to destroy any healthy relationships you have. They will also try to convince you to inherit their enemies.

Histrionics are master manipulators and take great pleasure in turning people against one another while they sit back and admire the results of their toxicity.

Five Proven Techniques to Help You Manage Your Emotions

Now that you know how to identify the major types of toxic people you are most likely to come across, it's time to master the techniques you need to protect yourself from their toxicity.

Let's face it: toxic people derive satisfaction from watching their victims succumb to their manipulations. They want to see you afraid, anxious, and depressed. They want you to doubt yourself, and they aim to lower your self-esteem. They will be observing your emotions for any signs that their plans are working. Therefore, you must thwart them by learning to manage your emotions. You must become a master of emotional regulation.

Contrary to public opinion, emotional regulation is not the same as suppressing your emotions or denying the way you feel. NO! Emotional regulation involves taking conscious actions to alter the intensity of any negative emotion you feel.

By mastering the emotional regulation techniques in this chapter, you can take control of your emotions and how you express them, and not experience emotions based on how others want you to feel. Emotional regulation enables you to deal with toxic people by starving them of the satisfaction they desire.

You can also use these emotional regulation techniques to free yourself of the consequences of any toxic influence you may be experiencing and start your journey to complete liberation and healing.

Here are the five emotional regulation techniques that you must master.

1. Identify and minimize triggers

2. Switch to positive self-talk

3. Select your responses

4. Search for positive emotions

5. Seek therapy

1. Identify and Minimize Triggers

It's impossible to completely avoid toxic people. You will need to deal with them regularly. However, you can minimize how often you need to deal with them. Handling negative emotions takes a significant toll on your energy levels, and the more you learn how to deal with them, the better things will be for you.

The first step to emotional regulation is examining past confrontations you've had to deal with and evaluating the events that led to them. Was it something you said? Was there a sign you ignored?

Identify the triggers that surrounded each event and led you to experience negative emotions and begin to remove them. To successfully identify emotional triggers, you will need to ask yourself serious questions and give honest answers.

Do not assume that everyone has the same emotional triggers. This erroneous assumption will hinder your emotional mastery. It is only by examining yourself that you will discover your emotional triggers.

2. Switch to Positive Self-Talk

It's common to berate yourself when faced with mounting criticism.

"I blew that!"

"I'm never going to get another opportunity like that."

"Maybe they're right; I'm totally useless."

Your words can shape your reality. If you continue to speak negatively of yourself, you'll reinforce these beliefs and strengthen their grip on you. Instead, treat yourself with empathy and replace such negative expressions with positive words.

"I'll find better ways to do that."

"If I try a different approach, I'll get the results I desire."

Understand that you must not become complacent by deluding yourself with falsely positive self-talk. It doesn't work that way. Recognize any areas in which you need to do better and make a commitment to improve. However, you should never talk yourself into accepting failure, guilt, helplessness, or any other negative emotions.

3. Select Your Responses

There's no denying that terrible things happen in life. Sometimes we are pushed beyond our limits and find ourselves confronted with awkward situations. Often, we give in to our natural inclination to lash out, scream our heads off, or even unload our aggression on the nearest victims. You must overcome that inclination.

Understand that you have the power to choose your response to any kind of provocation. Yelling, throwing tantrums, or other impulsive reactions might make you feel awesome at the time. However, if you indulge in those reactions, you will find that you end up with feelings of regret when the impulse passes.

Instead of subjecting yourself to such torture, take the time to pause and evaluate your response to any provocation. This not only applies when dealing with difficult people, but also when dealing with people in general. Speak calmly to people who offend you rather than yelling at them. Take the time to explain what's wrong with a colleague's work rather than unleashing abusive tirades.

Think about it for a moment. Reacting impulsively will likely ruin your relationships with other people and draw them into the vicious cycle of toxicity you should be trying to escape. Besides boosting your social credibility, pausing to choose the right response also improves your self-esteem.

In choosing the right response, you can apply the five-second rule. When provoked, delay your response for five seconds. This way, you overcome your impulsive reaction and are able to choose a better and more productive response.

4. Search for Positive Emotions

Humans tend to sway toward the negative. They will readily overlook any positive signs staring them in the face and seek out negativity, even in places where none can be found. This behavior is so common that a special name exists for it. It is known as the negativity bias. You can't blame them, though; negative emotions such as fear, anger, and anxiety carry a lot of weight. It's easy to notice them once they are present.

On the other hand, positive emotions such as peace, contentment, and gratitude are considerably lighter. You will only notice them when you make the effort. Begin to make that effort. Start by looking for the tiniest bits of light in overwhelming darkness. See the brighter side of every picture, and vocalize these feelings.

Your focus is your power. Whatever emotions you make the object of your focus will be amplified with time. By choosing to overlook negative feelings and focus only on positives, you maximize this power, boosting your mental well-being and improving your resilience.

5. Seek Therapy

Managing your emotions is not a feat that you can achieve all by yourself. You will need support and even professional help as you begin.

Although many people are born with mild temperaments, which they may have inherited from their parents, nobody is a natural expert at managing their emotions.

Like any learned skill, emotional regulation is mastered through constant practice. Managing your emotions requires a high level of self-awareness. You may find yourself overwhelmed by the effort, especially in the beginning. It is also more difficult to commit to emotional regulation in the face of mounting toxicity.

That's where therapy comes in. A professional therapist can help you discover better emotional regulation strategies, as well as evaluate your progress. Working with a therapist will help you to discover useful insights about areas in which you could improve your emotional regulation.

Takeaway

While it is impossible to completely avoid toxic people, you can identify them, measure your response to mounting toxicity, and create your escape route. By becoming a master of your emotions, you take back the control from toxic people around you and begin to put the necessary measures in place to protect yourself.

CHAPTER 2

The Deadly Affair

"Whoever conceals his transgressions will not prosper, but he who confesses and forsakes them will obtain mercy."

– Proverbs 28:13 ESV

We can better understand the trajectory of toxic abuse and the dangers of remaining trapped in the vicious web of toxicity by looking at the case of Emily.

When Emily met Jason, she believed her world was finally perfect. To Emily, Jason was the final piece of the puzzle her life had become. He was tall, well-built, and eloquent in speech. He was also doing decently for himself at his real estate firm. His voice had a unique tone that sent butterflies racing through Emily's stomach, and his eyes were so deep that she could lose herself looking into them.

Emily considered herself lucky. Jason was every lady's dream. They had met by chance at a sales fair. Besides his dashing looks, Jason had carried out his business with so much confidence that Emily found it increasingly difficult to hide her admiration. She had taken the initiative and approached Jason when the opportunity presented itself. They hit it off right away.

At first, their relationship sailed smoothly, but it wasn't long before Jason's true nature began to show through the flawless facade he'd presented to Emily. It started with a few harmless demands. He would ask for a random favor or a small loan from Emily, always providing a vague explanation for the request. Even though he never paid back any of the loans, Emily continued to give in to his demands.

Gradually, these little requests progressed into bigger demands and put a lot of pressure on Emily. Jason would show up unannounced to Emily's apartment with a few friends and stay as long as they wanted without the least concern for her comfort. He would have online purchases delivered to her address and made her pick up the items.

At this point, Emily had reservations about the relationship. Sadly, there wasn't much she could do. Jason was a master manipulator who was unafraid to use any of the trick cards he had up his sleeve. Whenever Emily objected to a request, he would unleash a venomous tirade on her. He even threatened to hit her on several occasions.

With time, Emily got to know more about Jason's dark lifestyle, including his history of drug abuse and his involvement in an offshore racketeering gang. Naturally, she was alarmed. As a laidback and easygoing person, Emily had never been faced with such a dilemma. She began to seek different ways to peacefully end her relationship with Jason. Whenever she tried to broach the topic, he would turn the tables on her, accusing her of being insensitive and trying to abandon him. He would sulk for days on end and gaslight her.

Soon enough, Emily began to doubt her sanity. She was sure she needed to end the relationship and that no good would come from staying with Jason, but every time she tried to face him, she ended up right back where she'd started.

One fateful day, Emily took the bull by the horns. She decided to abandon her apartment and take up new residence elsewhere. Unfortunately, Jason managed to track her to her new address and continued to torment her.

Emily felt completely helpless. Her confusion was further worsened by Jason's unpredictable nature. One moment he was all sweet and classy, and suddenly he was a raving lunatic.

She finally got her lucky break after Jason was identified in an ongoing investigation and placed behind bars. His incarceration allowed her to reevaluate her actions throughout their relationship. She discovered that she had lowered her standards just to accommodate Jason, and her self-esteem had suffered for it. All along, she had put his needs above hers. She had never put her foot down or challenged any of his toxic behaviors. She had always buckled in the face of any confrontation and blamed herself for everything that went wrong while they were together. She had become entangled in a deadly affair and lost the power to break free.

You might have a hard time understanding Emily's actions, but when you take a closer look, you'll realize that it wasn't her fault.

Emily is a typical example of a highly sensitive person. Her response to toxicity, which could easily be classified as irrational, was no fault of hers in any way. Many highly sensitive people never really make the effort to understand their nature and character traits. They excuse their responses. They try to suppress their reactions. They do their best to avoid confrontation. Ultimately, they play right into the hands of toxic manipulators and are left to rue their choices.

You do not have to make the same mistake as Emily. Being a highly sensitive person is nothing to be ashamed of. On the contrary, you should take pride in possessing a character trait that can only be found in 15–20% of the global population. By understanding your strengths and challenges as a highly sensitive person, you'll place yourself in a better position to effectively deal with high-conflict, toxic people like Jason.

How to Tell If You Are a Highly Sensitive Person

Just in case you're still wondering what it means to be a highly sensitive person, here you go.

A highly sensitive person (HSP) is an individual with an increased sensory perception of events around them.

Often, people refer to high sensitivity as sensory processing sensitivity (SPS). Whatever name you use, these people are more affected by events that others are quick to dismiss as insignificant. They pay more attention to details, see beyond the surface-level meaning, and are left with a deeper impression of things than others.

Being a highly sensitive person does not mean that you have a mental health condition. Not at all. There is no clinical diagnosis to determine highly sensitive people. High sensitivity simply implies a heightened responsiveness to any sort of influence, be it positive or negative.

As a highly sensitive person, it is common to hear other people telling you that you think too much or you're taking something too seriously. Oftentimes, you'll get such responses from toxic people who are seeking to dismiss your observations about their behavior or even turn the tables on you.

While there is no established diagnosis for high sensitivity, researchers have identified some prevalent behaviors that you could use to determine whether you are a highly sensitive person. You do not need to display all of these signs, or even more than one, to confirm that you are a highly sensitive person.

1. You reflect on things, a LOT!

HSPs have a hard time forgetting events. They will often replay events in their heads and criticize themselves for any failings they notice.

"Maybe I held on to his hand for too long when we shook hands."

"Should I have accepted that lunch invite?"

While these events may have no direct bearing or implications on the outcome of anything at all, HSPs will keep themselves occupied by imagining lots of different outcomes to these scenarios.

2. You can't function under pressure

HSPs are easily stressed. It is common to find HSPs freezing when forced to make the smallest adjustments to their schedule, or when they need to deliver an impromptu speech. They frequently blank out under mounting pressure or upcoming deadlines.

Understand that HSPs are usually meticulous, highly critical of themselves, and always strive for perfection.

3. You empathize with everyone

HSPs can easily detect the feelings and needs of the people around them. They take their time to view events through the eyes of every party involved. This behavior is a result of HSPs possessing more active mirror neurons.

It is quite common to find HSPs prioritizing the needs of other people above their own. They rarely hold toxic people accountable for their actions and make excuses for their behavior instead.

4. Your mind works on overdrive

There's hardly a dull moment with HSPs. Their brains are often racing, creating vivid stories and detailed pictures in which they can fully immerse themselves.

Besides overanalyzing every little event in their lives, they are creative thinkers with a heightened sense of self-awareness. The downside to this heightened self-awareness is that HSPs often end up criticizing themselves unduly.

5. You struggle with negative feedback

HSPs do not take criticism very well. They do not simply listen to negative feedback; they replay it several times in their heads and even fill in nonexistent gaps with words that were not even contained in the original feedback.

As they are highly analytical individuals and prone to self-criticism, HSPs blow even the slightest hint of criticism out of proportion. It is also common to find them going out of their way to impress others. They will do whatever they can to be in everyone's good books and avoid any form of criticism.

6. You ponder over every little decision

HSPs have a hard time making up their minds. Besides spending a lot of time trying to evaluate the possible outcomes of every decision they make, they also consider how their personal choices affect the way other people see them.

No matter how insignificant the decision might be, HSPs will do their best to identify the option with the lowest risk. They are full-time maximizers and believe that every decision carries lifelong consequences.

7. You notice every detail

Due to their heightened sense of perception, nothing ever escapes the notice of HSPs. Since they are very empathetic people and continually look out for others, they never fail to notice any signs that might give away others' emotions.

Continuous pen clicking, a casual glance, a slight pause. HSPs are quick to take in every detail around them. Unlike other people, HSPs are greatly affected by external stimuli. Hence, little details that seem insignificant to others might end up leaving them annoyed or overly excited.

8. You cry easily

Generally, HSPs are highly emotional. They get more overwhelmed by their emotions and often find it difficult to hold back the tears. HSPs usually avoid extremely violent movies and shows because seeing violence leaves them feeling unsettled. They will also avoid any events they believe might trigger intense emotions.

While many are quick to dismiss this behavior as that of a "crybaby," high sensitivity goes beyond that. It is not a sign of weakness, and it's certainly nothing you should be ashamed of.

How Toxic Relationships with High-Conflict Persons Affect You

Understanding why you react the way you do to the actions of toxic manipulators will help you break free of their grasp. Rather than allow them to prey on your high sensitivity, you can leverage your strengths instead, and put up effective measures around your space to limit their toxic influence.

Let's face it: highly sensitive people do their best to stay away from conflict. The very thought of confronting their toxic partners or work colleagues leaves them feeling extremely stressed. They would rather ride the rough waves of toxicity, hoping things will get better someday, and allow it to destroy their emotions and lives instead of putting a firm stop to it.

Here are some of the negative effects that you could suffer as a highly sensitive person in a toxic relationship with a high-conflict person.

1. Low Self-Esteem

The first thing toxicity does to you is reduce your sense of worth. Just like the venom of a spider paralyzes the unfortunate fly in its web, toxicity reduces your will to do something about it or even to take flight and get out of the situation. High-conflict people thrive in their toxicity when their toxic behavior goes unchallenged.

High-conflict people also continually put down the feelings of others. They have no problems with making other people feel useless or unwanted. This feeds their bloated sense of self-worth, and they continually strive to ensure that anyone who poses a threat to their ego is deflated.

You can tell your self-esteem has tanked when you find yourself constantly reviewing plans that you have perfected so many times already. Another sign is a constant feeling of inadequacy that plagues you whenever you appear in public (or even when you are alone). If you find yourself continually doubting your credentials or feeling like an impostor among your colleagues, understand that your self-esteem has taken a nosedive.

If you continue to allow yourself to be treated poorly, in time, your peace of mind and inner security begin to depreciate as well. You might even end up with a very poor personal relationship with yourself and continually subject yourself to harsh and undue criticism.

2. Constant Isolation

Due to constant self-doubt and greatly reduced self-esteem, you might begin to shy away from other people and to make up excuses for this behavior. But the truth is that continuous feelings of inadequacy will make you retreat into a shell or even build high walls between yourself and people who may want to help you.

You may feel constantly judged whenever you appear in public and remain fearful that others will see through you. Due to your heightened perception, you detect subtle criticism even in casual remarks and constantly mistake flattering comments for false praise.

Toxic relationships are a full-time job. They sap you of all your strength and leave you feeling drained. Therefore, you might find yourself too tired or unwilling to invest any effort into creating new relationships or maintaining existing ones.

3. Stress Disorders

Mounting toxicity subjects you to mental stress. No surprise there. Toxic behavior sparks the release of harmful neurotoxins that make you feel overly anxious, put you in a heightened state of alertness, and even make you feel depressed. If you have to deal with high-conflict people every day, whether they are mere work colleagues or your life partner, it will take a significant toll on you.

Besides constantly being on edge, feeling threatened, or feeling the need to defend yourself, other signs that could indicate you're experiencing a stress disorder include binge eating, oversleeping, feeling dull, and even talkativeness. Also, stress and anxiety disorders could push you into seeking dark or dimly lit spaces where you can hide away from bright lights to be left with your thoughts.

4. Constant Negativity

Due to their heightened perception, HSPs keep detailed records of any toxic abuse they experience. Not only that, their minds work in overdrive and continue to rehash graphic images of these negative experiences, magnifying even the smallest detail of the event. Frequent and uncontrolled contact with toxic people will leave you with fresh episodes for your mind to add to its library.

Toxic abuse leaves a heavy burden of negativity on your shoulders. Remaining under the burden of constant negativity will influence the way you see the world, the people around you, and even yourself. You will find it difficult to see otherwise. Since negative energy is often nearly impossible to shake off, you might become overly suspicious of those around you. You may doubt their motives and start to believe that they are all united in some grand conspiracy against you.

Ultimately, you'll begin to exude negative vibes to everyone around you and might find other people distancing themselves from you.

5. Heart Disease

In addition to your mental health, your general physical well-being suffers when you are subject to an unrelenting barrage of toxicity as well. There are no exclusions.

Research shows that people in toxic relationships are at great risk of suffering cardiac arrest, higher blood sugar levels, higher blood pressure, and heart problems. There's a basic logic for such occurrences. The human system has sufficient measures to protect itself in stressful situations. One such measure is "fight-or-flight" mode, which helps you come up with the desired response to any kind of stressful situation. However, remaining in a constant state of fight-or-flight takes a heavy toll on your immune system and eventually weakens your body.

6. Inadequate Self-Care

By now, you've probably realized that toxicity and negativity are opposite sides of the same coin. Toxicity breeds negativity and negativity leads to even more toxicity. When you are constantly plagued by negative emotions, you may find it increasingly difficult to keep up with your self-care routine. You may even give up on such routines entirely, whether that includes your regular workout, sleeping habits, or meal schedule.

Take the example of someone trying to deal with a recent heartbreak by lying awake all through the night, eating bowls of ice cream and basically turning into a couch potato. None of these actions will help them to recover from the breakup, but they can't help themselves because they're so overwhelmed by negative emotions.

Toxicity saps your energy and leaves you feeling drained. It could also reduce your sense of self-worth. Hence, you may find it difficult to keep track of previously established self-care routines; you may even conclude that they are no longer worth the effort. Ultimately, this lack of self-care leaves you in a worse state and makes you prone to even more negativity.

Remember, toxic personalities take great pleasure in tormenting highly sensitive people. To them, HSPs make for easy prey. They know that their toxic behavior will be unchallenged, and even when HSPs put some effort into confronting them, the toxic person can easily overcome such feeble attempts.

But it doesn't have to be like that for you anymore. Being a highly sensitive person doesn't mean you're a weakling who should let yourself be pushed around. It's time to put a stop to the toxic people who might be preying on your gentle nature. It starts by identifying the toxic people in your life. Below are the signs to help you identify whether you're dealing with a toxic person.

Eight Signs of a Toxic Relationship You Need to Know

Toxic relationships take a significant toll on you. Therefore, you should learn how to react to them or put a stop to them as soon as you notice them. You might be wondering if you're in a toxic relationship right now. Here are the telltale signs:

1. You face continuous criticism

2. You always walk on eggshells around the person

3. You feel constant guilt

4. You never receive an apology from them

5. You have no personal space

6. You never understand their behavior

7. You are constantly manipulated

8. You feel continually watched

Takeaway

If you are a highly sensitive person, it is impossible to deny or change your nature. However, you can limit the damage you suffer at the hands of high-conflict and toxic people by looking out for the signs you have learned in this chapter.

In the next chapter, we will discuss the effective measures you can take to create and maintain boundaries to protect yourself from toxic manipulators.

CHAPTER 3

Build A Personal Fence

"And the Lord's servant must not be quarrelsome but kind to everyone, able to teach, patiently enduring evil, correcting his opponents with gentleness. God may perhaps grant them repentance leading to a knowledge of the truth."

– 2 Timothy 2:24, 25

Imagine for a moment that you have been gifted a piece of real estate sprawling over hundreds of acres. It's all yours for the taking. But there's just one little problem.

Your property has no fence. There are no clear-cut boundaries to show you (and other people too) the limits of your newly acquired property. There are no restrictions to any unauthorized entry to this new property of yours. Anyone, I mean anyone at all, can casually stroll onto this property at will and do whatever they want, whenever they want to.

At this point, do you still believe the property is yours? Would you feel safe taking up residence there? Would you erect structures on that property? Without having any fences in place, there remains a limit to the kind of activity you can use the property for.

Without a fence, you could end up in a struggle for ownership of the property with future invaders. Without clear-cut boundaries, you would have a hard time suing any trespassers for encroaching on your property. Without a fence, you would leave the property at risk of misuse, abuse, and possible degradation.

So, what would you make a priority when you receive such a property? Building a fence! If you wish to secure your hold on that property and ensure that every investment you make on that piece of real estate is safe, you must put boundaries in place. There's no way around it.

Now that you agree that fences enable us to secure our property better, let's find out the most valuable piece of property you will ever have. It is impossible to place any form of monetary value on this piece of property.

Are you still wondering what this invaluable property is? It is your mind! This includes your mental well-being and your emotional health. You will never have any other property more valuable than your mind. In reality, the value of any other property you'll ever own is mostly influenced by your mental well-being. Therefore, you would be doing yourself a great disservice if you go above and beyond to secure less valuable properties but fail to pay attention to the most important one of all.

In the previous chapters of this book, we have examined the traits of toxic people, their methods of operation, and how to easily identify them. You have also learned the damaging effects that toxic relationships can have on you. In this chapter, you will master the art of setting boundaries to insulate yourself from toxicity and deter toxic manipulators around you.

Let's face it: toxic people never go away. You will always come in contact with them, even in the places you least expect. The only way to completely avoid toxic people is to hole up in a dark cave on some deserted island far away from human habitation, which certainly isn't very practical. However, while you can't avoid toxic people, you can moderate the amount of toxicity you have to deal with.

To highly sensitive persons, setting up these boundaries might seem extreme and unnecessary. However, you must remember that you need to prioritize your mental well-being. No, you are not being too harsh. You are not overreacting. You are not being rude or unhelpful. You are only establishing healthy boundaries that will let you get the best from your relationships and limit the influence of toxic people.

Effective Measures You Can Use to Define Your Emotional Boundaries

Setting up boundaries can be quite tedious for beginners. However, emotional boundaries are used to draw a line between the behaviors you find acceptable and those you do not.

Here are a few measures that you can begin with.

Say No

When faced with situations where you are forced to compromise on your ethics and principles, you must say no. Sometimes, you may try to play nice just because you don't want to offend those around you, and you may have a hard time saying no. However, you must make it a habit if you wish to send a strong signal to those who want to take advantage of you.

When you are faced with a decision that does not sit well with you, say no right away. Do not ask for time to think about it, or ask them to come back later for your decision. You are only leaving the door open for further manipulation. For example, if you are unable to work overtime, simply say no. Taking on more responsibility when you are overwhelmed will only put you under more pressure and cause you more stress.

Say no to impromptu events if you are not up for them. Also, turn down urgent demands that you know you'll have a hard time meeting. Once you've said no to unnecessary engagements a few times, other people will take the hint and adopt a better approach when they need your time and resources.

Reject Undue Blame

Do not take responsibility for other people's behavior. It is okay to understand the reasons for their actions, but encourage them to own up too. You may find yourself frequently taking all the blame just because you wish to avoid a confrontation. You must stop doing that. It is unhealthy and sets you up as a perfect trash bag for other people to dump all their nonsense into.

Whether you are having an argument with a colleague at work or trying to settle issues with your significant other, always try to identify your faults and own up to them, but never allow them to heap the blame for their actions on you.

"I spent your money without your permission because I found it lying around the house."

"I cheated on you because you always stayed at work too long."

NO! That's nonsense. Do not take that. Stop them immediately if they try to pin their failures on you. Never accept undue blame nor let it slide. Ensure that they take responsibility for their actions.

Dictate Your Feelings

Take power out of the hands of manipulators by refusing to let them belittle your feelings. This behavior is usually prevalent among narcissists and sociopaths, who will attempt to gaslight you into believing that your emotions are not what they seem and that you're just overreacting. This allows them to turn the tables on you whenever you confront them.

You have a right to feel any emotions you may be experiencing. You also have a right to express these emotions. Do not allow anyone to control the way you choose to express how you feel.

Declare Personal Space

Sharing an office space with several colleagues at work may diminish personal boundaries. However, you need to declare some personal space for yourself. This way, you ensure that you retain some sense of individuality. You also get to maintain some form of order around your personal belongings.

Other people might try to make you feel like a prude or an arrogant individual when you restrict access to your personal space. However, you should never allow anyone to make you feel guilty for drawing such personal boundaries.

How to Maintain Emotional Boundaries

Do not assume that the job ends with simply setting up emotional boundaries; that assumption would be incorrect. Now that you have identified the emotional boundaries you need and put the necessary measures in place, you need to maintain these boundaries, or all your efforts will have been for nothing.

Toxic people do not do well with boundaries. They believe they are entitled to unlimited and unhindered access to your life. Expect some form of resistance to the new boundaries that you have established for yourself. Setting boundaries is a gradual and tedious process, but one with long-term benefits. If you succumb to this initial resistance, you will never succeed in establishing these protective boundaries.

Here are a few techniques you can use to maintain and strengthen your emotional boundaries.

Be Clear

There should be no vagueness or ambiguity about your emotional boundaries. Set your boundaries out clearly so that everyone understands where you stand. If you feel the need to put these boundaries down in writing, go ahead and do so.

Just like an electric fence, your boundaries must be conspicuous. You do not need to shout them at those involved or constantly repeat them; however, you must bring any violations of these boundaries to the attention of the trespassers. Do this in clear terms to avoid a repeat of such violations in the future.

Do Not Compromise for Anyone

Never compromise your emotional boundaries for anyone or any reason at all. Compromising your stand is the fastest way to lose any sense of normalcy you might have achieved. If other people notice that you are willing to shift your boundaries for others, they will not take you seriously. Soon, you'll be forced to make so many adjustments that your boundaries become too vague to serve their purpose.

Remember that fences do not crumble in a day, but if you keep allowing people to pick your boundaries apart brick by brick, you will soon be left with no boundaries at all. Put your foot down. Give a firm but polite "NO" every time you are asked to make a compromise.

Live by the Rules You've Set

You also need to hold yourself to the same standard to which you hold others. That is the best way to remind others of the boundaries you have set. By continually living within the limits of these boundaries, you set an example to any violators who may attempt to test your resolve.

Remember that others will be constantly looking for ways to exploit any chinks in the armor in order to get past your emotional boundaries. Failing to set an example yourself is an open invitation to everyone. In addition, living by the same rules you've set for others helps you keep your boundaries in mind and ensure they are intact.

Remain Consistent

For your boundaries to work effectively, you need to be consistent. Turning your boundaries on and off is a no-no.

Fences that protect property owners against intruders never go on lengthy vacations or even short breaks. The same must be said of your emotional boundaries if they are to work effectively. So, no free passes, black Fridays, or happy hours. Your boundaries must be rigid and your response to violations must be consistent regardless of the scenario.

You might be tempted to let your guard down during holidays, nights out, or get-togethers, and simply slip back into character once that time has passed. NO! Emotional boundaries are not the same as light switches that you can casually flip at will. If you make it a habit to blur the lines whenever you wish, you will have a harder time convincing other people to respect your emotional boundaries.

Respect Other People's Boundaries

Finally, you must know that just like you, other people have emotional boundaries too. You are not the only one who needs to protect yourself. Try to identify other people's boundaries and relate to them within those boundaries. Also, take note of any observations people raise when you violate their established boundaries.

When you take note of other people's boundaries, you put yourself in a good position to demand that they respect your boundaries as well. Furthermore, respecting the boundaries of others reduces the likelihood of conflicts and results in more productive relationships.

Takeaway

Setting up emotional boundaries might seem like an uphill task from the onset. As you prioritize your needs and emotions above those of other people, you might feel like you're being harsh or inconsiderate when you notice their obvious discomfort with your new boundaries. However, you must not allow yourself to be swayed. With time, they will adjust. This is essential to building more harmonious relationships, void of stress and frustrations.

In the next chapter, you will discover 235 powerful phrases you can use to disarm invaders who may want to cross your boundaries.

PART TWO

Getting Started

CHAPTER 4

Powerful Phrases To Disarm The Manipulator

"A soft answer turns away wrath, but a harsh word stirs up anger. The tongue of the wise commends knowledge, but the mouths of fools pour out folly."

– Proverbs 15:1, 2 ESV

Susan was long overdue for a promotion at work. She had spent the past 11 years of her life working as a junior sales assistant at one of the fastest growing firms in her area. Before she joined the firm, her employers had struggled to achieve their annual targets. Their accounts had been in the red for several years in a row. They were about to close shop, throw in the towel, and simply sell to any available buyer.

With her resilience, strength, and wealth of experience, Susan was a much-needed breath of fresh air. Within a few months, she had established a sense of order within the firm and set the company back on track. Within a year, her employees were making plans to expand the business. Susan remained diligent and continued to shoulder most of the responsibility at the firm.

After a few years, the firm entered a profitable partnership that resulted in significant investment and more expansion. This upturn of events should have brought an improvement in Susan's fortunes, but that was not to be. The new investors considered Susan's methods old-fashioned and outdated. She never received any recognition for all her years of hard work and loyalty. Instead, they were trying to force her out.

Susan found herself at the end of verbal tirades and unrelenting barrages of criticism. She tried to make sense of the sudden change in attitude and seek clarity when the opportunity arose, but nothing she did or said changed a thing. Before long, she was regularly involved in shouting matches and verbal exchanges with her superiors and colleagues alike. Although no situation ever descended into a physical confrontation, Susan had prepared herself to accept that eventuality.

Just like Susan, you might be facing a similar situation at the office, school, or even at home. You might have overbearing family members who refuse to recognize the new personal boundaries you have set. Perhaps you have difficult colleagues who keep disrespecting you and continue to intrude on your personal space at work. Or you could have a manipulative partner who gaslights you, or maybe an overbearing boss whom you are finding increasingly difficult to handle.

Oftentimes, these people are unnecessarily difficult regardless of how reasonable you try to be with them. They will never give an inch of compromise. Rather, they will attempt to escalate tensions and pull you deeper into the murky waters of negativity. If you are not careful with your responses, you'll play right into their hands.

However, you can overcome such people by using the effective phrases in this chapter to disarm them. With these phrases, you can nullify potential threats, put a quick end to conflict, and save yourself from stress.

Effective Phrases for Disarming Toxic Manipulators and Diffusing Toxic Situations

1. I hope I haven't offended you in any way.

2. Would you like to discuss any issues with me?

3. Did something happen that I need to know about?

4. Have I said something you find inappropriate?

5. Is there something I've done to ...? If so, I'd appreciate it if you ...

6. If you have something against me, let me know. Otherwise, I expect you to treat me respectfully.

7. I won't engage in that kind of language. Tell me when you're ready for us to discuss this.

8. I think we need to talk about this ..., but only in a civil manner.

9. If we must have this discussion, you must treat me with respect.

10. I believe you have something to say about but it's difficult for me to understand what you're saying if you continue to speak that way.

11. Let's discuss this in a professional manner.

12. Comments like that are unhelpful, and only create negative feelings.

13. Please, don't describe me or my ideas as "stupid."

14. Comments like that are unprofessional and go against established ...

15. If you have some negative feedback about let me know privately.

16. Please, stop doing ...

17. You need to address me by my real name when I do not appreciate being called ...

18. I would like to but comments like that give me

19. I would like to increase ..., but constantly hearing how terrible a job I'm doing doesn't make me

20. We all try to ..., and embarrassing my team in front of ... destroys our efforts.

21. I would like to, but hearing that I'm notdoesn't give me a ...

22. I will not accept jokes about my partner or members of my family.

23. I would like it if you were more specific about

24. Please let me know how ...

25. What would you like me to do if a situation like this comes up again?

26. Let me know if I am getting this right ...

27. What signs of ... do you want me to look out for?

28. If I find the situation is getting ..., what would you rather have me do?

29. If we need to deal with ..., what do you suggest we do?

30. Because you raised your voice at the meeting, ...

31. You may have noticed that ... since you ...

32. Since you started calling people ..., they're not speaking out at the ...

33. After you called our plan ..., I can't get my team to

34. Since your episode with the ... last week, we have had to deal with ...

35. Does this idea sound like a good one to you?

36. Do I have your permission to go ahead with this one?

37. Let me know if you think this is a great idea.

38. Does this approach sound reasonable?

39. This seems perfect, don't you agree?

40. I will move forward with … if you say so.

41. It's okay to get started right away, right?

42. Let me get started right away. Are you okay with that?

43. Once you feel comfortable with this, I'll begin straightaway. All right?

44. As you instructed the other time, I …

45. I followed the same guidelines you provided last time.

46. Does this idea sit well with you?

47. Do you have any observations about our current progress?

48. Does this method look best to you?

49. You are clearly better at … Why don't you

50. Since you have mastered … so well, this little detail probably escaped your notice.

51. Because you're so busy, it's hard for you to

52. We know you're clearly better at this than

53. Given the fact you have a higher degree in …, you're clearly more suited for …

54. Since you're a big-picture visionary, you probably missed the …

55. I really enjoy … If you like, I can …

56. In my old position, I … for my boss all the time. Would you like me to … for you too?

57. I have a degree in … If you don't mind, I can review those …

58. I would really enjoy … before you …

59. If you like, I can … That way, you won't need to stress yourself over …

60. I'm not sure you realize this, but …

61. Are you aware that …

62. The … you gave was just what we needed. Just two observations I want to make …

63. Just so you know, I wanted to point out that …

64. You may not have noticed you said … when you probably meant to say …

65. Usually, we take these steps … Do you think we should change them?

66. Usually, the report includes … But we could make a few adjustments if you feel …

67. I was not aware that you saw it that way.

68. Thanks for letting me know how you feel.

69. I appreciate your input.

70. That's an interesting angle to take.

71. I understand what you're trying to say.

72. Thanks for giving me your input on this matter.

73. I see where you're coming from.

74. I find your observation quite interesting. You put it quite well.

75. I agree with many of the points you shared. Let's consider ways we can incorporate them.

76. You're correct in saying ... What do you think we should do?

77. Much of what you're saying is valid, so let's clarify some of these issues.

78. Yes, I agree. Actually, I'm meeting with the ... to discuss this issue.

79. I think you've raised very valid points. Let's make sure we are on the same page.

80. Instead of remaining at this impasse, let's find ways we can move forward.

81. How do you think we should proceed?

82. So what do you suggest we do?

83. I see what you mean. Now, what other issues would you like to discuss?

84. At this point, you need to be clear about the solution, not just the problem.

85. I want nothing to affect your progress, so it's best we address this issue.

86. Before you continue, we need to resolve one small problem.

87. You are all set to go. But if you focus on this aspect, I think you could improve your chances.

88. You need to remain a critical part of ... However, you should pay attention to ...

89. I would love to see you ... However, one small issue keeps getting in the way.

90. To ensure that you relate well with ..., I have to let you know that ...

91. To help you maintain your steady progress, ...

92. I must admit, I feel awkward telling you about this.

93. This is very uncomfortable for me to say.

94. This issue is somewhat personal—I feel weird bringing it up.

95. Normally, I shy away from discussing personal issues, but this is important.

96. I don't know how to say this, but …

97. I hope I'm not being too direct when I say

98. Please, don't take offense if I find it difficult to describe this situation, but …

99. Here's the issue we have to deal with. How do you think we can go about it?

100. We need someone who's really capable of handling … Think you can help us?

101. Which teams do you think would profit the most from your wealth of experience?

102. We can realize our target of launching this project in good time if you …

103. Last year, you were engaged in just …, but this year we need your expertise throughout the entire process.

104. Your past agrees that you are exceptional when it comes to …

105. We'd like you to help in these ways: …

106. I want you to take responsibility for … You are the best person to do it.

107. Last time, you helped the team complete … even though we were … We need your energy again this time.

108. Do you have anything you want to speak with me about?

109. Are you okay?

110. Are you having any issues with the …?

111. If you wish to discuss anything with me, I'll be at …

112. Is anything going on that I should know about?

113. I'd like an update on … What are your impressions so far?

114. Is there anything I need to know about how you feel about …?

115. I'm interested in your opinions, so please let me hear them.

116. You need to relax for a minute.

117. Calm down and let me know what you're thinking.

118. Take a few breaths before we continue.

119. Do you need some water?

120. Are you all right? Need a few minutes?

121. Why don't we sit down so you can tell me what you're thinking?

122. Let's look at the issues you raised and consider ways to address them.

123. Tell me exactly what's bothering you.

124. I know you have strong feelings about … I'd like to hear them.

125. What exactly do you have in mind?

126. I'm surprised to see you so upset—what's the problem?

127. I'd like to address the way you feel about this.

128. What did you mean by that last point?

129. I wasn't clear about what you meant when you said … Do you mean …?

130. Can you repeat your last statement—just so we are on the same page?

131. Did you or … actually say that?

132. Did anyone else witness the event?

133. How often do you think you are in this position?

134. I can see why you feel that way.

135. That's an interesting way to see …, and we should …

136. I'm sure other people feel the same way. Now here's what actually transpired.

137. I never knew you saw the situation that way.

138. That's a hard take. Now I see why you have such strong feelings.

139. That's exactly how I felt about …

140. Let me summarize everything you just said, and tell me if I'm getting it right.

141. I believe you said …

142. Am I right in assuming you meant …

143. Just to be sure, did you mean …

144. I want to understand you clearly, so please repeat that so I can be sure.

145. So here are … we can avoid … in the future.

146. I will get back to you about … within …

147. We agreed that you will …

148. You said that you would … Let me know if I can help.

149. So we can agree that …

150. What I understand so far is … Is that correct?

151. So we agree that … Is there something I missed?

152. This is what we are going to do about … Does that sound good to you?

153. I'll see what I can do about … Let me know if you come up with any ideas.

154. I see you're upset. Let me know what's wrong.

155. Why don't you calm down, and we'll see how we can resolve this problem.

156. Okay, relax, I'm here to listen.

157. I didn't mean to upset you. I'm sure we can resolve ...

158. Sorry, I didn't mean to upset you. This is what I meant ...

159. Why don't you relax while we try to figure this out?

160. Thank you for letting me know about this situation.

161. I appreciate you for sharing your concerns about ... with me.

162. Thank you for giving me the chance to resolve ...

163. Thank you for informing me of the situation at ...

164. Thank you for telling me about your experience.

165. I appreciate your taking the time to inform me about the ...

166. I am sure we can reach an immediate solution.

167. I appreciate the chance to clarify any misunderstandings.

168. I'm sure I can give an explanation for ... and come up with a good solution.

169. I need to hear what you have to say about

170. Your input gives me useful insight into solving this problem.

171. I know I can settle this easily with God's grace.

172. I can explain … to you.

173. I believe I can be of help.

174. Let me put that more simply.

175. I could show you how.

176. Let's go over … together.

177. Why don't we walk through … once again?

178. Just ask me any questions you have, and I'll do my best to clarify.

179. I apologize for …

180. I'm sorry about that you had to …

181. Sorry about the …

182. I apologize for the … Trust me, it will never

183. Sorry, this is taking …

184. I know this might look like a … Kindly bear with me.

185. I know you've been delayed for …

186. I'm afraid this is …

187. I apologize for the inconvenience.

188. This is … than I expected.

189. I appreciate your patience throughout all of

190. Thanks for waiting.

191. Thanks for remaining calm.

192. Glad we agree on … and that everything worked out just fine.

193. Hope you like this—I think you will enjoy it.

194. So nice to know you …

195. Thanks for your understanding.

196. I'm sure we can resolve this.

197. Don't worry, we'll find a way around this.

198. I think that's a fine approach, don't you?

199. Let's look at … together.

200. Just let me know what you feel the exact problem is, and we'll sort it out right away.

201. That must be really difficult for you.

202. Doesn't this … seem good to you?

203. I can understand why you have such expectations.

204. I see why you feel …

205. I can see why you need …

206. Yes, a lot of people feel the same way.

207. I definitely agree.

208. Well, that's very relatable.

209. Do you agree with …?

210. Does this … seem fair to you?

211. That's a fair compromise, don't you agree?

212. This is a reasonable solution, right?

213. That should work, don't you think?

214. Let me note down these objections right away. We could discuss solutions next week.

215. Thank you for raising that point. I'll address it in a few minutes.

216. That's an interesting point you made. Here's what you should consider …

217. What do you think we might have missed?

218. Thank you for bringing that up. We'll return to it later in this discussion.

219. That's a valid point—others have raised it too. Here's how things currently stand.

220. I'm glad you brought up that point—many people have made similar observations.

221. Yes, many people share the same view. The truth is that …

222. Thank you for sharing that view. I'd like to come to that.

223. That's an interesting point, but there's no sufficient proof ...

224. If you look at ... you'll find that isn't what occurs. However, ...

225. How do you think we could avoid these issues?

226. What do you think we should do, then?

227. What are some alternatives that could get us the same results?

228. Who do you think was correct in this situation?

229. What would you have done in that situation?

230. What kind of problems would this ... help you address?

231. When will you take the necessary steps to resolve this issue?

232. When have you witnessed similar scenarios at work?

233. Why do you think similar problems keep occurring?

234. I don't respond to that kind of language. When you're ready to speak, please let me know.

235. You must show me respect if you want us to continue this conversation.

Takeaway

When trying to resolve any kind of issue, timing is essential. Therefore, ensure it is a good time before beginning your conversation. If you find that the time isn't ideal for the other person, communicate with them to set a time that works for both of you.

PART THREE
Moving Forward

CHAPTER 5

Emotional Regulation

"This is my commandment, that you love one another as I have loved you."

– John 15:12 ESV

There is so much you can learn from veteran sailors, especially from those who have risen through the ranks to become accomplished captains of large maritime vessels. One thing you will always notice is their calmness, self-control, and mastery of their emotions. You'll rarely find them exploding in uncontrolled outbursts or losing their cool in the heat of provocation.

To casual onlookers, it is easy to assume that such behavior comes naturally with their job, or to simply give credit to their genes. While such assumptions may not be completely false, they only scratch the surface and paint an incomplete picture.

To better understand the reason behind the much-admired carriage of these professionals, let's take a look at the dominant element in which they work and draw relevant comparisons to our daily lives.

Many people agree that the sea can be a very treacherous place. And for some people, the mere prospect of traveling by sea can induce feelings of sickness, discomfort, and great fear. It is not a prospect for the fainthearted. Given that the sea is driven by great gales and continuously threatens to swallow anyone who dares approach, it is no wonder to find even the bravest of persons avoiding the sea if they can.

However, captains of large sea vessels never succumb to these fears. You'll find them as calm as ice in the worst of tempests while they sail through troubled waters. They never abandon their ships but remain accountable for the safety of every life and piece of cargo in their vessels.

Although their ship might be in great distress, and even in danger of mortal peril, the captain continues to give assurances to everyone on board as he radios for relief and gives instructions to members of his crew. Even if he is eventually forced to abandon the ship, he ensures that everyone aboard is safe and accounted for first.

You may be wondering how the captain can maintain his composure in the face of apparent dangers. How is he able to bravely weather these storms without ever giving in to his instinct for self-preservation? Is it possible that he has no emotions as normal people do? Or does he have some secret death wish? Not at all! The captain has simply undergone years of training that enabled him to master his emotions and dictate his responses when facing troubled waters.

If you wish to successfully deal with toxic people, you must begin to see yourself as a captain. Your life is just like a ship navigating through the troubled waters of toxicity, and you are the captain of that ship. You must be able to stay steady in the face of high tides and tempestuous winds that threaten to blow you off-course or even sink your ship.

Therefore, you must master the skill of emotional regulation. Just like the captain, you may have no power over the seas, but unless you remain the master of your ship, you won't be able to guide your vessel through the raging storms.

In the first chapter of this book, you discovered the five techniques of emotional regulation. In this chapter, you will discover the rules surrounding emotional regulation as well as the numerous benefits you stand to enjoy from mastering this art.

What Emotional Regulation Is All About

One of the most common misconceptions about emotional regulation is that it involves a suppression of our inherent instincts or a denial of our true emotions. That is not the case. Emotional regulation is a learned process that enables you to express your emotions in the way you desire. It involves mastering your emotions rather than allowing them to control you.

Emotional regulation refers to the conscious measures we take to keep our emotions in check.

At some point in your life, you may encounter challenges and become overwhelmed by your emotions, causing you to lose the power to offer the response you would like. At such times, you may find yourself acting out of character and in ways you are bound to regret later. You may also find yourself acting in ways that expose you to public ridicule and further manipulation by toxic individuals.

In dealing with toxic people, you must keep your emotions under control. This way, you disarm them, limit the influence of their toxicity, and ensure that you come out unscathed.

Remember, just like the captain of a ship, it is your responsibility to remain in full control of your crew members and ship even when you feel overwhelmed by the forces of nature. With emotional regulation, you can keep your emotions in check in the face of undue provocation, delay your response, and de-escalate toxic situations.

While many people can naturally regulate their emotions, those without this natural ability can learn and master emotional regulation skills. You only need commitment and constant practice. In addition to helping you overcome toxicity, emotional regulation benefits you in several other ways.

Three Scientifically Proven Emotional Regulation Strategies

While there are quite a few measures people take to calm themselves down when they feel overwhelmed by their emotions, there are three scientifically proven emotional regulation strategies that, if followed, will deliver exceptional results.

Attentional Control

This strategy involves intentionally shifting your focus and changing your perception of situations around you. Attentional control is simply overriding negative emotions by focusing on the positives instead. Instead of letting toxic situations weigh you down, you begin to look at them from a more constructive perspective.

For example, your senior colleague at work is talking down to you for no obvious reason. Your instinct may be to focus on negative feelings like anger, shame, and inadequacy that come with being put in such a humiliating position. However, you can come out on top of this situation by taking it as a sharp reminder to avoid letting that colleague put you in such a position ever again.

This way, you spare yourself the stress that comes from such episodes and prevent your self-esteem from taking an obvious hit. You also gain some insight into how to reduce the frequency of such episodes in the future.

Reappraisal

Reappraisal or reevaluation involves looking for better responses to situations that cause you emotional distress. With reappraisal, you dampen the impact of negative emotions in the short term while coming up with better ways to deal with such situations. Unlike forcefully suppressing the negative emotions you feel, reappraisal allows you to delay your initial response and offer a more measured response when you are out of the toxic storm.

For example, if you are confronted by a toxic partner who is yelling at the top of their voice over something insignificant, your first instinct might be to defend yourself and try to drown out their voice with your own. When you respond in this manner, you play into their hands and set yourself up for an energy-draining confrontation.

However, if you pause to reappraise the situation, you can identify their need for validation, act on that need, and quickly douse rising tensions without getting into a shouting match with them.

Self-Soothing

Self-soothing includes a number of activities you can use to reduce the negative emotions that toxicity makes you feel. Some of these activities include:

- Meditation

- Listening to music
- Breathing exercises
- Physical workouts
- Massage
- Cooking

The logic behind self-soothing involves the conscious adoption of healthy measures to overcome situations rather than allowing yourself to be overwhelmed by negativity and pushed into self-loathing and self-criticism. Note that all of these activities put you in a position to enjoy several long-term health benefits as well.

Purpose and Benefits of Emotional Regulation

The primary benefit of emotional regulation is noticeable in the short term (i.e., you will begin to experience less negative emotion in moments of conflict). But there are also long-term benefits to be enjoyed by committing to emotional regulation. Here are a few improvements you will notice once you begin to practice emotional regulation techniques.

Better Decisions

With emotional regulation, you can delay your response to a tricky situation and evaluate your choices. By adopting this approach, you take the steam out of heated confrontations and make improved decisions.

Walking away from an argument that continues to be illogical will save you lots of stress and possible physical harm.

Responding calmly to a brash colleague at work will douse rising tensions and ensure that group projects move at a quicker rate.

Rather than calling a toxic ex and crying over the phone, you can spend time with friends and other people who respect and value you.

Rather than taking to binge eating to cope with heartbreak, you can adopt a fitness routine.

While you may think that adopting a calm or nonconfrontational approach to potential conflict might make you appear weak, you need to understand that you are simply prioritizing your own well-being above that of everyone else.

Constructive Communication

Emotional regulation puts you in better control of your communication skills. Besides letting you pause and delay your response, it also allows you to put yourself in other people's shoes, see things from their perspective, and understand the underlying reasons for their actions.

For example, when dealing with a toxic work colleague who wishes to escalate a confrontation rather than reach a suitable compromise, it would be unproductive to argue with them or respond with counteraccusations. Instead, you can reply in a manner that makes them believe they are in control.

Remember, the key to overcoming narcissists and other high-conflict people is to let them believe they are in control. You can feed their egos and overcome them by telling them what they wish to hear without ever giving them any ground.

Improved Well-Being

Letting your emotions spiral out of control puts your health at significant risk. Allowing feelings of fear, worry, anxiety, and stress to become a constant feature of your daily life could also lead to depression and the development of other mental illnesses. By taking control of your emotions, you reduce the risk of mental health problems as well as the risk of developing harmful heart conditions.

When you regulate your emotions, you limit the impact of toxic situations on your mental well-being. You also reduce the frequency of events that could lead to the development of negative emotions.

Imagine a person who tries to cope with work pressure by drowning in several pints of alcohol at the end of the day. Or the person who resorts to doing hard drugs to cope with the pressure of unrealistic deadlines. In both cases, achieving emotional regulation would have allowed them to manage the stress that comes with their line of work by adopting healthier approaches. With emotional regulation, they could have also avoided taking on more responsibility than they could comfortably deal with. If they continue to handle work pressure by turning to substance abuse, their health will rapidly deteriorate.

Better Work Output

Emotional regulation improves your state of mind. Ultimately, this reflects positively on the quality of your work. When you are able to regulate your emotions, you reduce the frequency of downtime, which could affect the quality of your work or even stop you from doing any work at all. As you begin to master the various emotional regulation techniques, you'll discover that deadlines are no longer deadly nightmares that leave you scared and unable to function. You'll start to separate your feelings from work assignments and focus on the tasks before you without any emotional interference.

Besides giving you an improved outlook on your work, emotional regulation ensures you have better collaboration with your work colleagues. With emotional regulation, you can resolve lingering conflicts and nip potential conflicts in the bud, allowing group projects to move forward with relative ease and helping you to get more work done within the shortest possible time.

Increased Self-Esteem

Without emotional regulation, you'll find yourself getting the short end of the stick during any confrontation. You'll dwell a lot on negative emotions and give toxic manipulators more control over your feelings. Continuously putting yourself in such situations will cause your self-esteem to take a significant hit.

Lack of emotional regulation will also cause you to give wrong responses to conflict situations. You may find yourself yelling, using swear words, or even engaging in physical confrontation because you let your emotions overwhelm you. In addition to leaving you with cringeworthy episodes that are too shameful to look back on, such outbursts affect your credibility with others. As a result, you may find yourself constantly plagued by self-criticism, self-doubt, and low confidence.

However, when you have mastered your emotions, you'll reduce the occurrence of such events, control your response to them, and come out on top. You'll be left feeling generally better about yourself, and your self-esteem will improve.

Healthier Relationships

With emotional regulation, you can improve the quality of your relationships. Besides helping you to communicate effectively and handle conflict better, emotional regulation gives you self-awareness and confidence that lets you command the respect of others. By mastering emotional regulation skills, you'll discourage high-conflict, toxic people from engaging you in unproductive confrontations.

Emotional regulation also helps you to foster a more positive outlook on life and the people around you. It makes you more empathetic and observant of situations and empowers you to remain cautious while engaging potentially toxic people without being overly suspicious. This will positively affect the way you relate to people and help you build healthier relationships.

Takeaway

Emotional regulation changes your perception of toxic situations and gives you better control over your emotions. By practicing these skills regularly, you'll increase your self-esteem, improve your relationships with others, create healthy boundaries, and limit the harmful influence of toxic people.

Conclusion

Toxicity is not something you can wish away. You will probably meet toxic people at home, in your workplace, and even in random public spaces. It is impossible to control other people's behavior, but it is entirely possible to control your response and determine how much their behavior affects you.

In dealing with toxic manipulators, you must leave nothing to chance. You need to master the various techniques that will enable you to identify the deadly traps of toxic, high-conflict people, regulate your emotions, and memorize the key phrases you can use to disarm them.

You are taking a great risk by expecting toxicity to simply roll off your person like water off a duck's back. If you continue to expose yourself to negative emotions without mastering emotional regulation techniques, you put your mental and general well-being at risk. Your self-esteem will also suffer in the long run.

However, you can save yourself from all that trouble by adopting the proven techniques you have discovered in this book. With God's help, you can become the captain of your ship as you sail through the turbulent waves of toxicity. You can become an expert at disarming toxic people and stripping them of any control they might have over you.

By taking your choices out of the hands of vicious manipulators, you will become empowered to create a new world—a world where you define your perceptions and opinions. A world where your feelings and emotions do not depend on other people's validation. A world where you are in control of your space. A world where you thrive without constant criticism, doubt, fear, or guilt.

Thank You

I hope you enjoyed this book on dealing with difficult people. Now it's time for you to go and implement these techniques in your life for your personal growth.

If you haven't yet, check out my other books on Amazon for much more regarding your personal development for a happier and more fulfilling life.

Click here to view my books on Amazon:

https://www.amazon.com/Robert-JCharles/e/B092DLKRYH?geniuslink=true

References

- Benjamin, S. (2007). Perfect Phrases for Dealing with Difficult People. New York: McGraw Hill

- Evenson, R. (2013). Powerful Phrases for Dealing with Difficult People. New York: AMACOM

- Jarai, M. (2022, February 10). What is a highly sensitive person? Medical News Today. Retrieved from https://www.medicalnewstoday.com/articles/highly-sensitive-person

- Klynn, B. (2021, June 22). Emotional regulation: Skills, exercises, and strategies. BetterUp. Retrieved from https://www.betterup.com/blog/emotional-regulation-skills

- Lue, N. (2010, June 22). Boundaries in relationships: Understanding your personal electric fence. Baggage Reclaim with Natalie Lue. Retrieved from https://www.baggagereclaim.co.uk/boundaries-in-relationships-understanding-your-personal-electric-fence/

- Miltimore, J. (2018, March 6). Five types of people who can ruin your life in a hurry. Intellectual Takeout. Retrieved from https://intellectualtakeout.org/2018/03/5-types-of-people-who-can-ruin-your-life-in-a-hurry/

- Waters, S. (2020, July 22). The role of emotional regulation in life (and work). BetterUp. Retrieved from https://www.betterup.com/blog/the-role-of-emotional-regulation

- WebMD Editorial Contributors (2020, December 2). Signs of a toxic person. WebMD. Retrieved from https://www.webmd.com/mental-health/signs-toxic-person

www.ingramcontent.com/pod-product-compliance
Lightning Source LLC
Chambersburg PA
CBHW070440130626
46553CB00006B/2264